Contemporary Music of Japan

PIANO CONCERTO [score]
KINOSHITA Makiko

現代日本の音楽

ピアノ・コンチェルト [スコア]

木下牧子

音楽之友社

ONGAKU NO TOMO EDITION

Piano Concerto
by KINOSHITA Makiko

Ⅰ ········· 3

Ⅱ ········· 41

Ⅲ ········· 69

INSTRUMENTATION

2 Flutes (2nd doubling on Piccolo)
2 Oboes
2 Clarinets in B♭
2 Bassoons

2 Horns in F
2 Trumpets in C
2 Trombones
1 Tuba

Timpani
4 Percussion players
1-Maracas, Wood Block, Snare Drum, Bass Drum, Cymbals, 2 Suspended Cymbals, 2 Cowbells, Xylophone, Marimba,
2-Triangle, Suspended Cymbal, Glockenspiel, Vibraphone, Tubular Bells,
3-Bass Drum, Snare Drum, Suspended Cymbal, 2 Cowbells, Maracas, Triangle, Xylophone, Marimba

Solo Piano

Strings

〔Duration : ca. 18 minutes〕

初演：2012 年 10 月 16 日　東京オペラシティ コンサートホール
　　「オーケストラ・プロジェクト 2012」
　　指揮：大井剛史　　管弦楽：東京交響楽団
　　ピアノ：永野光太郎

the first performance of the original version:
16 October 2012 at Tokyo Opera City Concert Hall
Orchestra Project 2012
Conductor: Takeshi Ooi, Tokyo Symphony Orchestra
Piano: Kotaro Nagano

改訂初演：2019 年 6 月 19 日　東京オペラシティ コンサートホール
　　「木下牧子作品展 5 〜オーケストラの時」
　　指揮：大井剛史　　管弦楽：東京交響楽団
　　ピアノ：岡田 奏

the first performance of the revised version:
19 June 2019 at Tokyo Opera City Concert Hall
KINOSHITA Makiko Works V　Orchestral Time
Conductor: Takeshi Ooi, Tokyo Symphony Orchestra
Piano: Kana Okada

Piano Concerto
ピアノ・コンチェルト

I

木下牧子 作曲
Composed by KINOSHITA Makiko

18

24

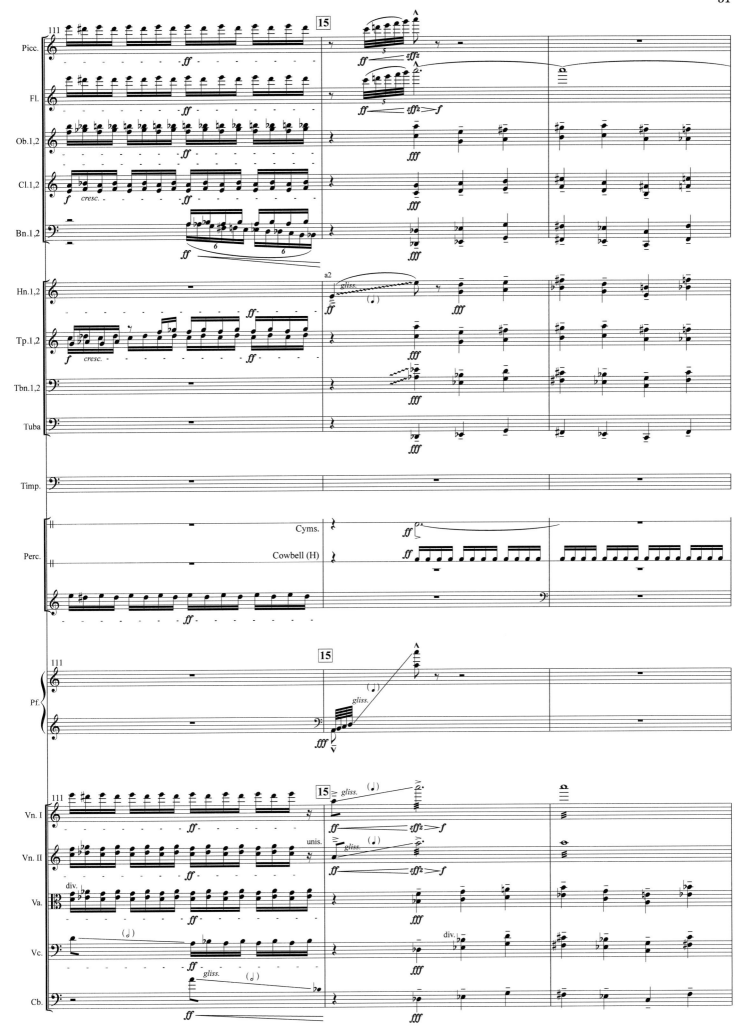

32

36

II

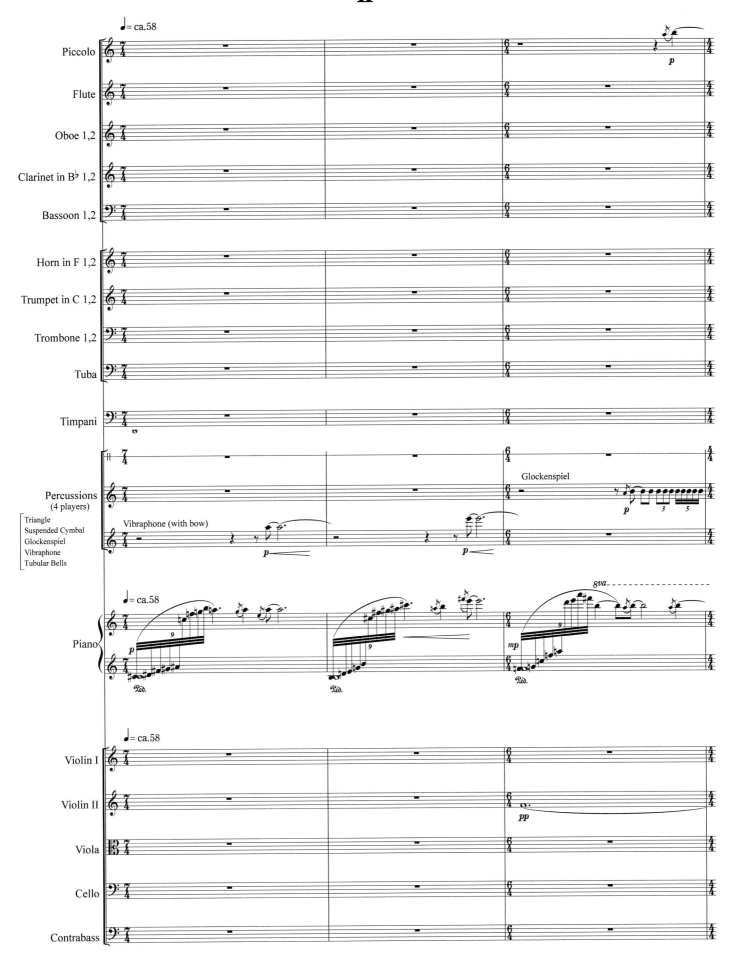

44

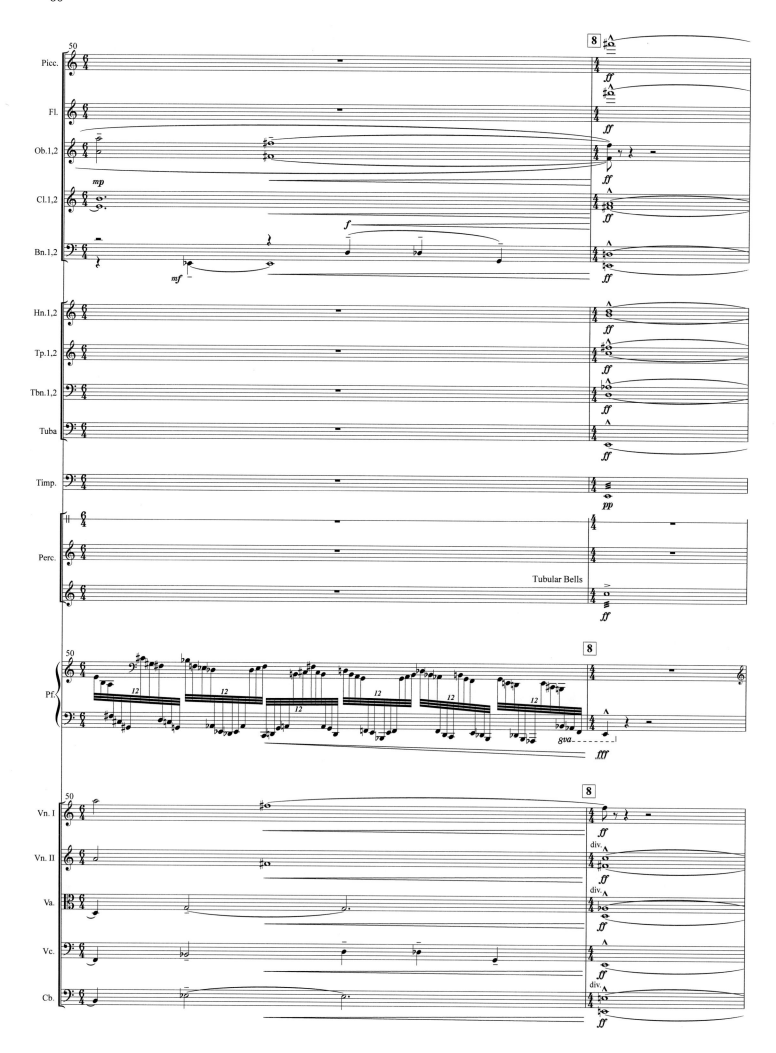

61

III

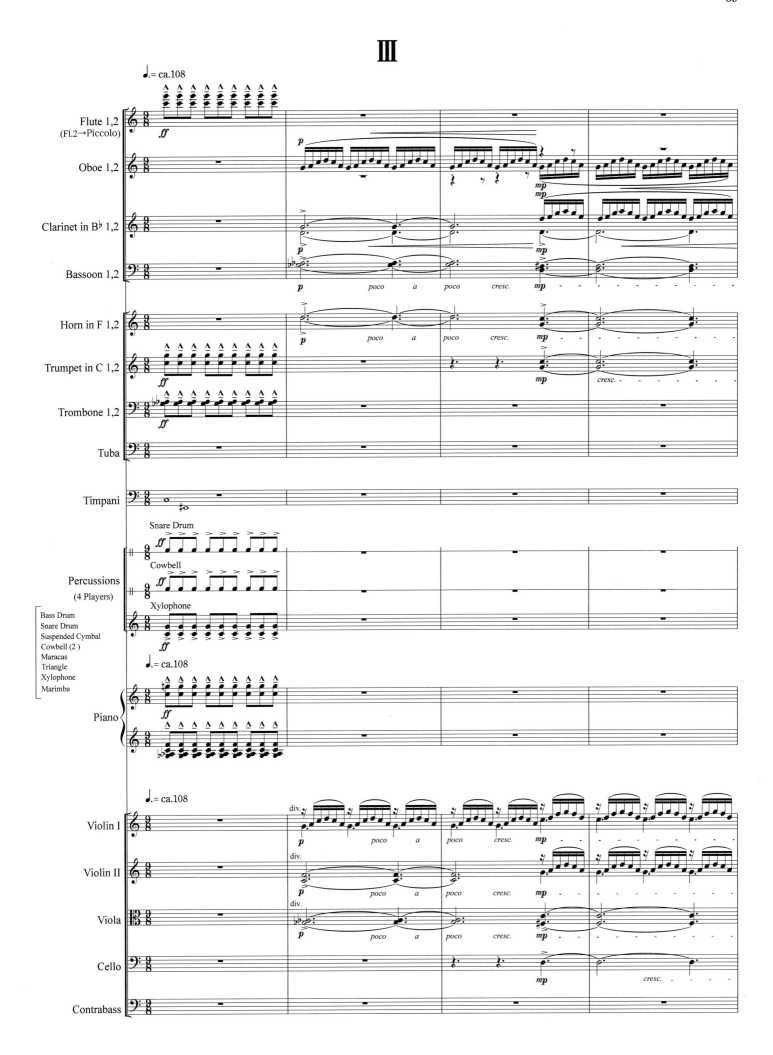

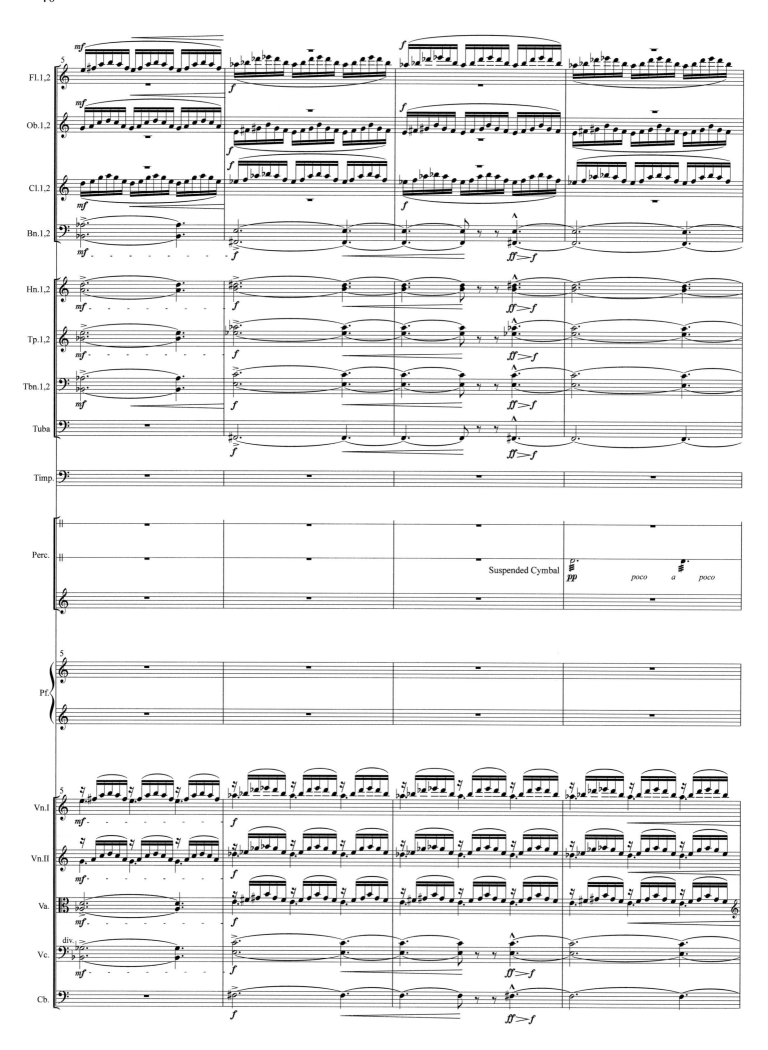

76

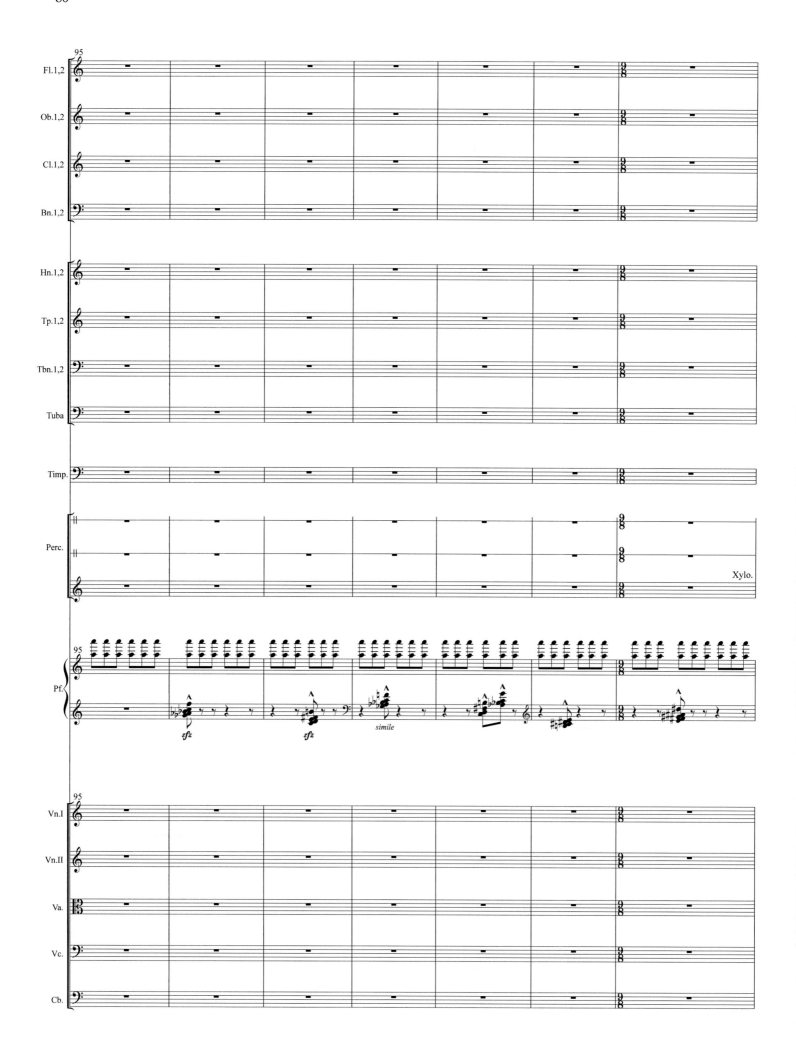

104

110

ピアノ・コンチェルト

　2010年に久々のオーケストラ作品を発表したところ、予想以上に評判が良かったため、引き続き2012年に《ピアノ・コンチェルト》を発表しました。初演後、音楽之友社から出版のお話を頂いたのですが、編成の大きい器楽作品は、必ず再演（改訂）してから出版することにしているので、涙をのんで再演の機会を待ちました。7年後の「木下牧子作品展5〜オーケストラの時」において、ようやく納得のいく改訂初演を行い、スコアを音楽之友社から出版頂くことができました。出版にあたっては、音楽之友社の中澤 慶さんに大変お世話になりました。

　初めてのコンチェルトなので、熟知する楽器・ピアノを選びました。この作品を書くことで、日頃便利に使っているピアノが、いかに奥深く可能性に溢れた楽器かを再認識することができました。オケは平均的な2管編成。現代オーケストラ作品は（自作も含め）長大な1楽章形式が多いですが、この作品では3章にはっきり分けることで、各章の対比を打ち出しています。同型反復を基調とした明快な構成とオーケストレーション、協和音程を多用した色彩的な響きの中に、ピアノという楽器の魅力を最大限に引き出したいと考えました。

2019年6月
木下牧子

＊パート譜と指揮者用スコアはレンタルで扱っております。問合せは下記へ。

㈱音楽之友社 著作権管理室：〒162-8716　東京都新宿区神楽坂6-30
Tel. 03-3235-2116　Fax. 03-3235-2110
E-mail: copyright_dept2015@ongakunotomo.co.jp

Piano Concerto

　In 2010 I completed a work for orchestra, my first for several years. Encouraged by the unexpectedly favourable reaction that it received, I set about composing a piano concerto, which was first performed in 2012. Ongaku No Tomo Sha Corp. immediately approached me with regard to its publication, but it was my principle only to publish a work for large instrumental forces once it had been performed a second time and I'd made any necessary revisions. I thus anxiously awaited the subsequent performance. The revised and definitive version finally received its premiere seven years later at a concert of my orchestral works, after which Ongaku No Tomo Sha Corp. kindly agreed to publish the score. Special thanks are due especially to Kei Nakazawa of Ongaku No Tomo Sha Corp. for her efforts in this connection.

　This was the first concerto I had ever written and as the solo instrument I chose the piano, the instrument with which I'm most familiar. Working on the piece, I realised once again the enormous depth and range of possibilities offered by this instrument that I use for convenience on a daily basis. The instrumentation incorporates standard double winds. Contemporary works for orchestra, including my own, tend to consist of a single extended movement, but I structured this work into three clearly separated movements in order to establish a clear contrast between the main sections. My intention was to bring out to the full the attractions of the piano within the context of a clear structure and orchestration featuring formal repetition and colourful timbres making extensive use of consonant intervals.

June 2019
KINOSHITA Makiko

＊The parts and the conductor's score are available from the publisher on rental.
ONGAKU NO TOMO SHA CORP., Copyright Department
Phone. 03-3235-2116　Fax. 03-3235-2110
E-mail: copyright_dept2015@ongakunotomo.co.jp

皆様へのお願い

　楽譜や歌詞・音楽書などの出版物を権利者に無断で複製（コピー）することは、著作権の侵害（私的利用など特別な場合を除く）にあたり、著作権法により罰せられます。また、出版物からの不法なコピーが行われますと、出版社は正常な出版活動が困難となり、ついには皆様方が必要とされるものも出版できなくなります。
　音楽出版社と日本音楽著作権協会（JASRAC）は、著作者の権利を守り、なおいっそう優れた作品の出版普及に全力をあげて努力してまいります。どうか不法コピーの防止に、皆様方のご協力をお願い申し上げます。

株式会社 音楽之友社
一般社団法人 日本音楽著作権協会

LOVE THE ORIGINAL
楽譜のコピーはやめましょう

〈現代日本の音楽〉

ピアノ・コンチェルト［スコア］

2019年7月10日　第1刷発行

490918

© 2019 by ONGAKU NO TOMO SHA CORP., Tokyo, Japan.

落丁本・乱丁本はお取替いたします。
Printed in Japan.

作曲者　木下牧子
発行者　堀内久美雄
発行所　株式会社 音楽之友社
　　　　東京都新宿区神楽坂6の30
　　　　電話 03(3235)2111(代)　〒162-8716
　　　　振替 00170-4-196250
　　　　https://www.ongakunotomo.co.jp/

翻訳：ロビン・トンプソン
印刷／製本：錦明印刷(株)